# Save It or Spend It?

## by Maureen Blaney Flietner

Editorial Offices: Glenview, Illinois • Parsippany, New Jersey • New York, New York

Sales Offices: Needham, Massachusetts • Duluth, Georgia • Glenview, Illinois
Coppell, Texas • Sacramento, California • Mesa, Arizona

# The World of Work

Do you get an allowance? Do you get money as a gift? Many children get money in these ways. You earn money by working at a job or doing chores. Money that you earn is called income. There are many different kinds of jobs in the world and many ways to earn money.

You can earn money at jobs by providing services or goods. Services are the jobs that one person does for another. Goods are things that people make or grow and then sell.

## What Can You Do with Money?

What do you do with the money that you have? Many children in the United States like spending their money on toys or dolls or snacks. Spending is one thing you can do with your money.

Spending is not the only thing you can do with your money. Putting money into **savings** is even more important. When you save money over weeks, months, or years, your money adds up. If you can save $10 each week, your savings would add up to $40 in four weeks and $90 in nine weeks! Watching your money add up can be fun!

# What Do You Need to Live?

A need is something a person must have in order to live. Food, clothing, and shelter all are needs.

There are some people in the world who do not have enough money for their needs. Some people cannot find jobs. Some people are sick and cannot work. Some are old and some are children. They may not have clothes, shoes, food, or other needs. Others try to help these people take care of their needs.

## So Much to Choose From, So Much to Want

A want is something you would like to have, but that you can live without. It can be hard to tell a need from a want.

How do you know if it is a want or a need? Fancy shoes or special jeans might seem like something you cannot live without, but you can. They are wants, not needs.

Businesses would like you to buy their goods and services. They advertise to tell you about their products. You can decide if you really need them.

# Plan Ahead

Do you look forward to doing something special? Are you thinking about the future? That is how you should think about your money. What do you want to do with your money next week or next month?

Think about how much money you would have if you saved everything you earned until next month or until next summer. What would you do with it all? When you think about how you will use your money, you start to plan.

| Saving for a Bicycle | |
| --- | --- |
| Week 1 | $10 |
| Week 2 | $10 |
| Week 3 | $10 |
| Week 4 | $10 |
| Week 5 | $10 |
| Week 6 | $10 |
| Week 7 | $10 |
| Week 8 | $10 |
| Week 9 | $10 |
| Week 10 | $10 |
| Total | $100 |

# Make a Money Plan

You can plan ahead by making a **budget**. A budget is a plan for your income, spending, and savings. It can help you decide how to use your money to meet your needs and wants, both now and in the future.

What if you wanted to make a budget to save for a bicycle that will cost $100? Let's suppose your total allowance and job earnings add up to $10 a week. If you saved all $10 each week, it would take you 10 weeks to save enough to buy that bicycle.

You may save $5 each week and spend $5 each week. It would take you 20 weeks to save enough to buy the bicycle. Do you want to wait 10 weeks or 20 weeks? You decide.

# Budgets Work for Families, Too!

A budget can help you learn to save and to spend. A budget can help families plan for their needs and wants.

Think about what a family needs. It needs money to pay for a home, heat, and electricity. It needs food, a stove, and a refrigerator. Family members need clothes.

A family also has wants. Everyone might want a television set or a computer. A budget will help a family decide how much money it has and how much it can spend.

# Smart Choices Help Everyone

If you have more needs and wants than you have income, you will not be able to pay for everything. That is why you need to make smart choices about money.

One smart choice is to think of ways to save more money or to spend less. Instead of spending more money by going to the movie theater, a family can spend less money by renting a movie and making popcorn at home.

When you find ways to save, you often help people besides just you and your family. When you turn off the lights that you are not using, your family spends less on electricity. You reduce the need for coal or gas. Coal and gas are **nonrenewable resources** used to make electricity. Their supply is limited and they cannot be made again. They are not like **renewable resources**, such as the wind, or water and sun power, that can be made again.

## Making Choices

You make choices each day. You also have money choices. Save or spend? Buy this or that?

You might go to the store to buy a music CD, but also see a video. They both cost the same. You decide to buy the music CD. You have chosen one item instead of another and made an economic choice.

Do you remember our sample budget? If you buy the music CD, that will change the bicycle budget. It will take longer to save enough money to buy the bicycle. You decide to continue to save for the bicycle.

## Supply and Demand

Almost every year, there is a new toy that is very popular. Everyone seems to want it. There is a **demand** for it. Once the **supply**, or number available, is gone, there are no more of those toys to buy.

Months later, there is a new supply of the toy. Now there is much less demand and the toy is on sale.

You decide to buy the toy at the lower sale price. You can still save some of your money and have that special toy too. You often can get what you want for less money. You can spend and save too!

## Learn About Your Choices Before Spending

In our sample budget, you are saving for a bicycle. You should learn about your choices to know which bicycle is best for you. You can go to the library to read about bicycles. You can visit stores to look at bicycles.

You finally decide on a bicycle. The company that makes them has resources, such as tools, machinery, and buildings. It also has people who know how to make the bicycles. The company brings in some of the bicycle parts it needs from other countries. The company's bicycles are sold to other countries. This buying and selling between different countries is called international trade.

# Your Budget Is a Success!

The big day is here! You have saved $100 to buy your bicycle. Your parents will pay the few extra dollars needed for the tax. A tax is money that the government takes. Taxes can help pay for the services of police, firefighters, and teachers.

You give your $100 to the owner of the bicycle store and get your bicycle. Later, the owner uses your money to pay the salespeople and the people who make the bicycles. The owner also pays the company that made the bicycle parts and the tax to the government. The owner keeps the profit, or the money left over after all costs are paid.

The money you spent for the bicycle now goes to many people. They then use the money they earned to pay for their needs and wants. They spend money on goods and services, and they save. Their money then goes to other people.

People depend on other people. The bicycle store owner depends on workers to make bicycles. The owner depends on people like you to buy the bicycles. The bicycle company workers depend on the company owner to give them jobs so they can earn money. Other store owners depend on their workers and the people who will buy goods and services from them. Everyone depends on each other.

# Make Smart Choices and Reach Your Goals

We made a sample budget for a bicycle. You can make a budget for a real goal. It can be a goal for a want or a need. It can be a goal to help someone. Pick a goal!

Next, you must decide how much you want to save each week. The more you save, the sooner you will reach your goal. You must also decide how long you want to wait to reach your goal.

Follow your budget! Sometimes it can seem hard to save. You may miss out on some other things you might want. When you reach your goal, you will be happy you made a budget and stuck to it. A budget can teach you how to make smart choices about your money.

# Glossary

**budget** a plan for your income, savings, and spending

**demand** the number of goods or services that people want and will buy at a given price

**nonrenewable resources** supplies that cannot be made again

**renewable resources** supplies that can be created naturally

**savings** money you have kept for future use

**supply** the number of goods or services that producers are willing to make at a given price